The Twins:

Royce and Boyce

Our Story of Survival and Adventure

By Boyce Reginald Moudy

The Twins:

Royce and Boyce

Our Story of Survival and Adventure

Copyright

Table of Contents

Dedication

I dedicate this to my twin brother, Royce, my mother Sweetie, my children, and to all that have the special bond of a love that lasts beyond a lifetime.

Acknowledgements

I wrote this about 20 years ago. I am now 86. I don't know why I would write it and just sit on it. I have had a good life, had three children, and they have all been successful. I have been single for about 23 years. I met this young lady about a year ago and I mentioned I had written about my life. She is an editor and wanted to read what I wrote. She loved it so much she has helped me bring this story to life and helped me publish it. I can't thank Betty Norlin, with What Is Holistic Health, enough. She is wonderful and I love her. My memory is not what it was, but everything is the truth. I hope you find it easy reading.

Prologue

This is a true story of twin brothers growing up in rural Texas in a sharecropping family. The youngest sons of a mixed marriage. They were the youngest of six children: Billy Gene, Charles Houston, Joanne, Donald Wayne, and the twins Royce Edward and me, Boyce Reginald. We were nearly change of life babies since there were nine years between us and the next oldest. It is also about the love of our lives, Sweetie, our mother.

Our story will not cover our siblings, because they had left home by the time this story takes place. It focuses on our true story, the hardships we endured from an alcoholic Indian father, Willie Corben, the love of a wonderful mother, Allie Odell Nelson, who everyone

called Sweetie, and the devotion and protection of one

twin brother to the other.

Chapter 1: Sweetie and the Twins

My mother was born in Texas near the Oklahoma line. She was the youngest of three children. Her father was a school principal and teacher. Her family was very close to each other, probably because they were very religious growing up on a farm. Growing up on a farm meant there was always work to be done. They had 500 acres of land that was farmed by sharecroppers. These were people, usually families, that farmed the land for a share of the profits. The children of these families worked at the farm before and after school. Most of them never finished high school. They usually got married at the age of 15 to 17.

This was a hard way to make a living. The owner would foot the bill to farm the land. After the sharecropper worked it all year and brought it to harvest, they would split the profit based on a percentage agreed upon. If the crops and profits were bad, the sharecropper had nothing to live on and everything could carry over to the next year. It could mean that the sharecropper could be in debt for years if a family wasn't lucky with good weather. Their life could still be enjoyable with a comfortable living and food on the table. Livestock was a big part of these farms, and the cropper could own his own cattle and horses.

Families worked together in the fields. The sun determined everything: when to go to work, when to stop for dinner, and when to eat supper. Dinner at noon meant the mother would go home and half an hour later the farmer would follow. After he had dinner, he would lie down on the floor with the hammer in his hand over his neck. When he fell asleep the hammer would fall and wake him up. He would then return to work.

Farmers grew or raised everything they needed except flour, sugar, and sometimes lard. The farmer butchered his own cows, pigs, chickens, and sometimes turkeys for all the family meat. Every month or so a traveling store would come by with flour and sugar. Flower was bought in 50 LB bags. The bags were made of material that was used to make shirts and some pants.

The gardens could be as big as a half-acre. Fruits and vegetables were grown. A lot were canned. Cows and pigs were butchered, smoked, and stored in a smokehouse. Wood was a big item because wood stoves were used for food. Wood was burned under water and boiled to wash clothes. It was then rinsed in hot and cold water.

One enjoyment people had in the summer was with baseball. Teams would meet on the weekend and play tournaments. Sweetie and her sister would attend these games, when they could sneak away from their parents. It wasn't that easy since the games were on Saturday. Saturday was a religious day for their family. People did not know my mother's family was Jewish.

Sweetie had heard about a new boy that had started playing for one of the newer teams. When she and her sister arrived at the game, they sat in the seats on the third base side because the new boy played left field. When the game started, she couldn't get a look at him, since he was so far away. In the third inning a foul ball was hit near her. As he ran in, she finally saw him. He

4

had jet black straight hair, brownish skin, and dark eyes. As he fielded the ball, he stopped in front of her. She stared at his dark reddish face. He was so handsome. As he caught the ball, he stopped in front of her and yelled, "You are a real sweetie." That is how it all began.

Chapter 2: Sweetie and My Dad

Nothing more was said until after the game. He was handsome—but it was evident he was an Indian. After the game all three of them, my mom "Sweetie," her sister, and the new boy, sat and talked. He told them he was from Oklahoma, but in the summer, he came to Arkansas and Texas to play ball in their tri-state league. He had black hair and dark eyes. My mother was immediately attracted to him, even though she knew it was wrong. He said he was playing the next day and could she come and watch him. She said she would try.

She asked her sister not to say anything to their father, he being as strict as he was. When they arrived home, she did something she had never done before.

She lied to her father about where they had been and done that day. Sweetie said they had taken some food and books and spent the afternoon reading. Sweetie told her father they planned to do the same thing the next day.

That night in bed, Lorine, her sister, was furious with her. "I can't believe you lied to Papa." "I had no choice, if I told him the truth, he would be furious and prevent us from returning to the ball field." Lorine did not want to return, but after much pleading from Sweetie she finally agreed. When they arrived at the ball field the next day, the game had already started. He was a very good ball player and really was the leader of his team.

As he came by between innings, Sweetie asked him a question. What is your name? As he went to the field he yelled "Corben." At the end of the game the three of them sat in the shade and talked about their lives. Corben said his mother was full blood Cherokee and had died when he was very young. His father was a sharecropper, and they were moving to Texas or Arkansas to find work. Things had not been good in Oklahoma. The farm they had been working on was sold and his family was forced to move on.

Sweetie knew this should end, but she was so attracted to him she couldn't end it. Her father had sharecroppers and might possibly have some land for them to farm. Her sister immediately spoke against this idea. Finally, it was agreed that Corben's father would approach her dad for work and nothing else be said. And when they left each other that afternoon she knew this was wrong, but she couldn't help herself.

On their way home Lorine was very upset. "How can you send a **** ***** Indian to work for our father?" "I like him," Sweetie said. "You can't be serious. He is half Indian and do you know who we are. We are a Jewish family. What do you think Papa is going to say about this?" "I have no intentions of telling him right now," Sweetie said.

As the weeks passed, Sweetie was attending the games without her sister. At one of her visits, he told her that his father had worked out a deal to sharecrop for her father. She was overjoyed. This meant they could be near each other and could continue their meetings.

When summer came to an end the ball season was over, they would sneak out at night to see each other. One night she did not come home. When she arrived home the next day, Corben was with her. She remembered what her mother said, "God will protect you if you truly love someone."

When they walked into her home, she immediately saw her father. Before Sweetie could say a word, her father demanded they leave his house and never return—that she was no longer his daughter. Sweetie's mother began screaming, "Please no Abi, don't do it." She burst into tears and stormed out. Sweetie was crying. She loved him, but nothing could be done. As she left her home and went immediately to Corben, she told him exactly what happened. Corben asked her, "Do you truly loved me, because that's all that matters." She said, "Even though I have only known you for a short time, YES! I know I love you."

Chapter 3: Young and In Love

She now became the wife of a sharecropper. They were very happy. Sweetie worked with him in the fields daily. The sad part of her life was that she did not have contact with anyone in her family. On occasions Lorine would sneak over and visit. That became so painful when she had to return home that they agreed not to put themselves through such agony.

Corben, along with his dad, were hard workers and the farm did very well their first year. Sweetie became pregnant with my oldest brother during their second year of marriage. After my two older brothers, Billy Gene and Charles Houston were born, Sweetie became pregnant with my sister, Joanne. It wasn't an easy pregnancy, because Sweetie continued to work even while she was pregnant. When she gave birth, it was assumed her mother would come and help. It didn't happen. Her dad had forbidden it. It was very hard for Sweetie. Her family was forbidden from having any contact and having a hard pregnancy made it more difficult. Thank goodness it turned out to be a normal birth.

After the birth of my sister, times were good. Mom became pregnant again with my brother, Donald. The bad thing was, Sweetie had no contact with her family. Six years passed and still no contact with her family, but she and Corben had prospered. They were allowed to purchase land from her father even though Sweetie had no contact with her family.

Chapter 4: The Twins

On September 1938 Sweetie became pregnant with the twins, Royce and me, Boyce. Again, it was not an easy pregnancy. My twin was sickly at birth and needed both breasts to nurse. We had a Negro lady who helped Sweetie. She too had a small child and nursed me for a spell. She was a wonderful big lady with large breasts that gave lots of milk. Thank G-d for her.

Sweetie and Corben were a happy couple. They had six wonderful children; their farm was doing well, and they were a couple in love. She never heard from her family. Even though her parents did not live that far away there was never any contact. Corben had business with her father from time to time, but her dad never asked about her or his grandchildren.

It was extremely hard on Sweetie not hearing from or seeing her family for years. She would from time to time see her sister, Lorine. Corben tried to make her happy, but he could see how she had been hurting. After all, they were married as young teenagers when they were both kids and, in those days, people never moved far from their family, even after marriage—but she was happy with her six children, especially the twins.

We were her pride and joy, even though the birth took its toll. Sweetie had been advised not to have another child; it could be fatal. All of a sudden, she seemed to change after the twins. Not toward her children, but it affected her relationship with my dad. The affection she had always shown toward him was not there. She seemed to resent having to work on the farm, while taking care of the family and house. We were happy boys. My brother was sickly and demanded most of the attention, yet he seemed to be getting stronger month by month.

As he grew older, he naturally had questions. "Why did the family down the road have two grandparents, when we only had one grandfather?" Sweetie always explained that our other grandparents lived so far away it was impossible to visit them.

Life was wonderful. She had two growing boys and an older daughter and a loving husband. Her three other sons were already grown and out of the house. She stopped working on the farm with Corben to take care of her children.

Sweetie had a piano that was given to her by her mother. Even though she could only play by ear, we would sit for hours at night listening to her playing and singing. If we could hum the song, she could play it.

Chapter 5: The Still Change

Things started to change when our neighbor and my dad began experimenting with moonshine. They even erected a little still that started out as a hobby—to make whiskey for personal use, but it became a full-time job. People drove from miles around to buy this clear alcohol. Things were fine until my dad began drinking every day.

I have heard that Indians can't control alcohol. If that is true, it certainly was so with my dad. He became a changed person when he drank. It seemed to make him violent. He would accuse people of talking about him and when this happened, he became violent. Sweetie was accused of trying to date other men or talking bad about him. As a result, arguments would break out. Sweetie never wanted us to see this, so we were sent outside to play while this was happening.

We returned home from school one day to find her with a black eye and bloody lip. I will never forget the look on my brother's face when he saw our loving Sweetie with her face swollen and red. He couldn't stop crying, even though she told him she had fallen.

We had many jobs to do—whether it was milking cows or feeding chickens and gathering their eggs. When I think back on those times, I remember we never wore shoes in the summer unless there was a special occasion. In the fall Sweetie would order our shoes and coats from the Montgomery Ward catalogue. We thought nothing about not wearing shoes because no one else did.

The Twins: Royce and Boyce

When we outgrew the shoes, Sweetie would give them to the Negro family that worked for Corben. We played and we ate dinner at the Negro's house. The only difference was, at night they went home if we were playing at my house, and we did the same if we were at their house. I loved listening to them singing their Gospel songs. There was such meaning. What I remember about them when I was growing up is that you never knew if they were rich or poor, they were always happy and so polite. It is a shame what has happened to this country. There were no mixed marriages because they were against it as much as we were. Life was so simple then. Life was wonderful.

Dad had let the farm deteriorate the last few months, but he began working to catch up. Sweetie seemed to be happy, but still cold around my father. My brother and I were always busy doing something. We had horses and cows to take care of, but to us it was full joy because at night we had our Sweetie to play the piano and sing to us.

It always seemed that good things can come to an end. Even as small boys, we could see this happening.

Chapter 6: Drinking Changes Things

Corben arrived drunk one night and immediately started arguing. Sweetie tried to quiet him down for the sake of the children. My sister, who it seemed was never home that much, cried. He finally passed out after going to sleep. Sweetie put us to bed and asked us to calm down. She told us that everything was fine. It was impossible for us to relax. After crying ourselves to sleep, we woke up with a start because of loud talking and yelling. Royce, my twin brother, immediately started crying. He jumped out of bed and ran into our parents' bedroom.

When I finally caught him, he was standing next to our parents' bed. We thought our father was hurting our Sweetie, because she kept screaming "Get off me." Little did we know he was forcing her to have sex. When she saw us, she screamed, "Oh no!" I grabbed my brother and pulled him back to our room. I felt so sorry for him. I could not stop him from crying.

I've always believed our childhood had an effect on him. Even as we grew older, he always hung around our mother. Growing up as a twin meant a lot. Even though my brother was sickly until he was about 10 or 11, he was a great companion. We were very good in sports and participated in all the school activities. Our father encouraged us to excel even if it meant missing work on the farm. But he had started drinking again. One afternoon at baseball practice, he arrived drunk. He began criticizing the manager, who was also one of our teachers.

Finally, this teacher asked him to leave. After arguing with the teacher, he took us out of practice, and we went home. We never returned to play ball again.

Because of his drinking, the farm work was not being done. We had laying hens that had to be cared for. My brother and I fed the chickens and picked up the eggs every day. Most of the cows took care of themselves, except the ones that had to be milked. Some of the days our dad helped us, but there were days he was nowhere around. When that happened, it was very difficult to finish everything.

I don't think people realize the effect it can have on small children to never know what condition your father is going to be in when he finally comes home. Money became very scarce, which forced my dad to start selling our chickens. He discovered one day he only had a hundred of the original 500 left. Panic set in and forced him to make a decision. He decided the family would move and pick cotton to earn money to bring the farm back in line. Years later it dawned on me that my father had more hairbrained ideas than anyone. We loaded everything we thought we would need for the summer and headed to find a farm to pick cotton. Corben mentioned to Sweetie that it appeared she was gaining weight. She didn't think it was funny and she didn't laugh with the rest of us.

After a day or two, we found a cotton patch that was hiring. The farmer was glad to hire a family to pick cotton. He even had a two-room shack. The only problem was, both rooms had a hole in the roof. My brother and I thought this was great! We could stare at the moon and stars at night as we were falling asleep. We discovered the downfall of a roof with a hole in it— when it rains—you get soaked.

Sweetie started gaining weight and she finally told my brother and I we would have a new baby in the house, but she never seemed to smile. It was a side of her that my brother and I had not seen. We were accustomed to her smiling face while she was hugging us. She only had a two-burner kerosene oven to cook from, so all the food was usually fried. Even though she had no stove to cook from she would somehow make us a little cake when she could. She would work in the field but would leave about 12 to fix dinner. About an hour later she would bring it to us where we were picking cotton.

One day she never came back. After an hour or so, we all went to see what happened. We found her lying on the floor, blood was running down her legs. She was as white as a sheet. I don't know who I felt the worst for—Sweetie or my brother. I cried for her, but I also cried for him. He threw himself on the floor next to her and was screaming, "Sweetie, Sweetie...Please don't die!" We didn't know what a miscarriage was. My dad ran to the farmer's house and returned with the farmer and his vet. He assured us that she would be OK. He also brought this Negro lady to help my mom. I thought she was wonderful. Years later it occurred to me that this wonderful black lady reminded me of the one who nursed me when I was small.

It was the first time dad showed any emotion. He even allowed my brother to sleep next to our Sweetie. She would hold him until he fell asleep. I never realized until years later how sensitive and delicate my brother was. I always blamed it on the fact that he had been sickly when he was a baby and how he always depended on our mother for support and that extra love. We headed back to the farm expecting to resume where we had left off. Our family worked all summer and earned $1,000.

Things were different when we returned. Corben had not let my grandfather know we were leaving for the summer, and he would not be paying on the land he had purchased. As a result, another family was living in the house. The 10 acres had been foreclosed on and we no longer had the land. We were lucky enough to be able to move into another house and had some furniture. My dad had no problem finding farm work. Farmers were always in demand. The downside was they usually drank there after work, and he would arrive home loaded.

We were getting older now. Our sister had left home and married a man from Waco, TX. My brother and I were attending school and were well adjusted in our way of life. Sweetie was still our precious mother. My brother was not as sickly anymore but still dependent on her. She finally took a job at a cafe in Marlin, a small town not too far from where we lived. She would bring home cakes twice a week for her two boys. We earned extra money from selling pecans on the side of the road, because the family needed the money. Sweetie started coming home later at night, being driven by the cafe manager. She would tell my dad about having to work late. By the time she arrived, he was nearly drunk anyway. My brother would stay awake until she arrived and only then would he come to bed. Even as a grown man, I would catch myself crying thinking about how he so loved his Sweetie. All of a sudden, she became more affectionate. Everyday telling the two of us that she would always love us no matter what happened.

Corben began hanging around the restaurant where Sweetie worked. He would stay at least four to five hours taking up her time and annoying the regular customers. It reached a point one evening when he arrived drunk. He began annoying the customers and the manager had to ask him to leave. When Sweetie arrived home that night, she told us what had happened, and it might cost her the job. The next morning, she approached him with the problem. He was sober then, and that meant he could be reasoned with. Sweetie told him that our family needed the money to live on and if he continued showing up, she would lose her job.

Children aren't stupid. They know when there is a problem, and we knew there was one in our home. Our parents never smiled and never seemed to talk to each other, but our mother always had a smile and loving word for us. She would even bring a treat for her Trixie, my brother's dog. Trixie was a mongrel who seemed to have a litter of pups every year. We never had any problem getting rid of them because someone always wanted a dog.

The last litter she had were all females and no one wanted them. As much as we tried, we couldn't find any takers. My dad brought the two of us together and told us that we had to get rid of the puppies. I said, "Dad, no one wants any female pups." He said, "I know that. I want you two boys to take them into the woods and bang their heads against a tree until they are dead. I know this is hard, but it will help make a man out of you." I thought my brother was about to faint. He started to scream, "No!" as he began to cry. I knew he would never be able to do this horrible thing. He ran to the puppies as if to defend them, which made our dad very angry. Just before my dad began to spank him, I yelled, "I'll do it!"

When I think about this today, I can still hear the puppies yelling as I held them by the tail and crashed their heads against the tree. That affected me the rest of my life. I was crying as I carried each one in a separate cage. When I came home, my brother asked if I had killed the pups and where were they. I couldn't stand to tell him the truth. I told him I had given them to this Negro family that lived near us. That day lives with me even to this day. From then on, we locked her up when she went into heat. It was hard to explain how hard we worked as boys. We would wake up in the morning, milk the cows by hand, and then feed the chickens. I never really thought that much about the work we were doing. All children of farmers were accustomed to doing a lot of work.

We also had enjoyment. Our enjoyment came from simple things. If we weren't fishing, we were hunting. Every young child back then knew how to shoot a rifle and clean whatever they killed. The Negros killed many armadillos for food. The dogs would chase them until they caught them. Then they would turn them over where the soft spot of their body was and then kill them. They had to stop the dog from biting the armadillo too much or he would make it impossible to clean.

The first time I ate a cooked or barbecued armadillo I was told it was chicken. I told them it didn't look or taste like chicken, but it was very tasty. When I heard it was armadillo, I didn't know whether to smile or throw up. The way it was cooked was different. We ate different things people would not eat today. We did have days we pretended we were either Cowboys or Indians and fought the good fight. Sometimes we wished our lives had been easier and simpler. We were good boys and just wanted a happy home, but I guess that couldn't be. Times were really getting hard. Corben wasn't working and the only income was coming from Sweetie. Sweetie's job as a waitress was what supported us. Whatever money Corben earned he usually spent it on Lone Star beer.

My dad, my brother, and I finally got a job working for Ernest Radle. At 12 years old I was raking hay. My brother and dad were working on a hay bailer. The work bailing hay was especially hard work. The hay would blow over you and the dust would get in your eyes and nose to the point you could hardly breathe. It was so bad my brother could hardly breathe at night. I asked Mr.

Radle if I could trade jobs with my brother because it was very hard for him to sleep at night. He agreed provided my brother could rake enough to stay ahead of his three bailers. I trained my brother how to cheat a little on the widest of the rows of hay. In those days bailing hay had two people on the bailer—one to push and one to tie the bales of hay. Even though I would sneeze at night I was glad my brother was getting a good night's sleep.

Mr. Radle was a good man. The only problem was he loved to drink beer. This was right down my dad's alley. After work each day the men who worked for him would sit and drink beer together until it got dark. My dad would take us home and make something for my brother and I to eat. Sweetie would still be at work. My dad became a very good chef serving spam and pinto beans. To this day I throw up thinking about spam. The ones who really loved this dish were our dogs. We were seeing Sweetie less and less because we were always working on the farm. When she came home at night, we were already asleep, but she would come into our room and kiss us good night. I can still feel her kissing my cheek even though I was asleep.

Chapter 7: The Great Parent Escape

One of the last nights I can remember was hearing arguing from her bedroom and I heard her yelling as she ran into the kitchen. I heard a large bang and someone hitting the floor. When I ran into the kitchen, Corben was lying on the floor. She had knocked him out with a skillet. I just turned around and went back to bed. I knew something was wrong. We were thirteen years old and soon to be 14—and Sweetie was always late coming home. But even though we had gotten bigger, we were still her babies, and she was still our Sweetie.

One morning when we awoke, she wasn't there. My brother began to cry saying, "Where is my Sweetie?" It always hurt me to see him cry. I could never understand why I felt that I was responsible for him. When my dad threatened to beat him if he didn't shut up, I said, "Dad he only wants his Sweetie." He slapped me across the face. I grabbed my brother and took him outside before we really got into trouble.

Corben said he knew where our mother was, and he was going to get her. He told us to go to work and tell Mr. Radle that he was sick, and he would try to be there the next day.

When we came home that night from work the house was dark and empty. We waited an hour or so until I found a match and lit the lamp. I lit the wood stove to heat up the kitchen and also to fry some potatoes and eggs. As we sat eating supper my brother kept asking me if I thought Sweetie was on her way home. I convinced him to go to sleep and he would see her in the morning. I always found it odd he never asked about our dad.

When morning came and no Sweetie, he became panicky. Not only was there no Sweetie, but our father wasn't there either. I'm glad he had Trixie; she kept his mind occupied. We still had work to do. He had some chickens that had to be fed and two cows to milk. When we went to work that day, I asked Mr. Radle, "What highway goes to Houston?" He drew me a map and the highway to take. He wanted to know how our father was doing. We told him he was sick but would be back to work in a day or so.

We kept busy around the farm because there was always something to do. The hardest time was at night. My brother was always looking outside to see if Sweetie was coming home. I would hold him at night as he cried himself to sleep. We were finally eating persimmons and eggs. I laugh about it today, because these persimmons were not even ripe.

Chapter 8: The Great Twins Escape

I told my brother we would have to leave—our sister was married, and her husband was in the Air Force stationed in Houston. We agreed to leave in two days. In preparation there were many things that had to be taken care of. I had a prize DUROC boar pig that had to be returned to the Future Farmers of America. My brother had a white-faced bull which also had to be returned. I really wanted to leave in about two or three days, but I didn't know if we would be able to. Nights were the worst for the two of us. We were running short on kerosene for light until Mr. Radle delivered some.

I can remember our dad singing two old songs to us when we were eight or nine years old. One was *Two*

Little Boys and the other was *Boys in Blue.* When I had children of my own, I sang these songs to them and believe it or not they sang the same songs to their children.

When we were alone at night we would sing these songs. These were soothing for both of us. The one I really liked was *Two Little Boys.* I often wondered why the old songs told a story and were so sad. We sang these songs before falling asleep. I don't know if we prayed. I hope we did. We were two young boys who were lost and had no direction. We often said, "Please Sweetie, come back to us" so I guess that was our way of praying.

Thank goodness for the chickens providing us with eggs. I came up with a great idea. I would slaughter a chicken, heat and boil some water, and then cut the inside and clean it. Then boil him again—that way I could clean all the feathers off before I cooked him. I remember seeing my dad wringing the chicken's neck and then smacking it until the head came off. Then you could clean it. I began ringing its neck, but I couldn't kill the chicken. All I did was make it mad. I dropped the chicken, and it began chasing me around the hen house. I quickly decided that was not such a good idea. So, we ate eggs and persimmons.

We packed our two old suitcases. We discovered they were broken, so we had to tie a rope around each one of them until they closed. The day before we left, I brought five dozen eggs to Mr. Radle, and he paid me $3. I thought I was rich. I finally told him we were leaving the next day, and he could have the chickens and the livestock because we had no one to take care of them. He asked us to stay with them until our parents returned, but I had decided we had to leave and find our sister. He also agreed to take my brother's dog. That night I think I held my brother until we awoke the next morning. We were already packed when Mr. Radle came back to take us to the main highway.

He put our suitcases in the back of the pick-up, and tried to change our minds, but I said, "No." I asked him to tell our parents that we would be at our sister's house in Houston. Right before he dropped us off, he handed me two more dollars and told us only to spend it for something to eat. When he dropped us off it was early in the morning. It was a beautiful day. The sun was shining, and the weather wasn't too hot.

We didn't have to stand on the road very long before we got our first ride. We threw our suitcases in the back of the pick-up and climbed inside. Our driver was a very talkative man who was full of questions. He wanted to know if we were brothers because we didn't look like brothers. When we told him where we were going, he couldn't stop laughing. He thought we were kidding. I assured him we weren't. Because we were in farming country our rides were only a few miles. We were tired, moving the two suitcases from ride to ride really took the energy out of us.

Chapter 9: Adventures on the Road

We had walked about a mile and the sun was starting to go down. We stopped at a bar and purchased two Baby Ruth candy bars. After eating the candy, I noticed people playing shuffleboard. It appeared they were all drunk. I will never forget the name of this place. It was named "The Y Inn." I kept watching, and this idea came to mind. We watched people play and when we saw the two most intoxicated people, we challenged them to a game. We decided we would bet them our $2.00 and we would double our money when we won. We challenged a man and a woman to a four-man game. They were so drunk it was hard for them to stand up. I bet them $2.00. I knew we could beat them. As they came to the board, neither one could hardly stand up.

The only problem was my brother, and I had never played this game. We were allowed to practice because we were young. I told my brother to just keep it on the board. The game started and I quickly saw we were in trouble. They knocked us off the board every time. I quickly realized if you don't know how to play, you're in deep trouble. Needless to say, we lost. I did not think two young boys would have to pay for a game that we lost to these drunks. I was mistaken. They not only took our money but wanted to know if we wanted a rematch. Nobody seemed concerned that two young boys were in a bar at night.

As we went outside to get our suitcases, I noticed it was getting dark. I told my brother we would have to stop somewhere because we couldn't see where we were going. We came to a bridge in the road, and I knew it was time to stop. We left the road and crawled under the bridge. I know my brother was as afraid as I was. I couldn't let him see that I felt the same way he did. We crawled underneath the bridge and found a spot. We had to get some sleep because we had a long way to travel the next day.

We opened our suitcases and laid them in front of us. We laid down in front of our suitcases and rested our head in the open cases, as if we had a pillowcase under our heads. We slept next to each other and talked about the way Mr. Radle took our dog Trixie and what we should do after we found our sister. I don't know exactly what time it was, but I could feel and hear the rain.

After a few minutes the rain was coming down so hard it washed us from under the bridge and we were floating down the stream. When we finally stopped, we had moved about 100 yards. It was cold and we were soaking wet. Luckily the suitcases were still together. We pulled the suitcases out of the water and laid them under a small tree. I don't know how long we slept but we were soaked.

While we were there, as I looked at my brother, I could feel his pain. I never realized how fragile he really was. How he missed his mother and how totally afraid he was. When we awoke that morning, we were hungry and soaking wet. We dragged our suitcases out to the highway and began hitchhiking. There were very few cars on the road, and it seemed as if it was slow for over an hour. One of us would sit on the suitcase while the other one thumbed.

We didn't realize it was Sunday morning and people were not working. All of a sudden, a car stopped. It was a man, a woman, and a young girl. He was dressed in a suit and the woman and little girl had nice dresses on. The little girl was probably our age—cute and a great smile. The man opened his trunk to allow us to put our beat-up suitcases away. We were wet, dirty, and smelled like mold.

He asked us where we were headed, and we said, "Houston." As he chuckled, the lady said, "You have to be kidding." I replied, "No, we have a sister there who will take care of us." It had never dawned on me as to how I was going to find her—I just knew we had to get to Houston. I didn't consider the mileage or the hardship to get there. I guess I was too young to think about that. My main thought was taking care of my brother and getting to our destination. We were really tired and kept dozing off when the lady said, "Did you give thanks to Jesus today?"

Now, you have to understand that my father was an Indian and my mother was Jewish. We knew who Jesus was but never gave thanks to him for anything. To this day I never have forgotten my brother's answer. He said, "For what? Our parents left us. We are wet, cold, and hungry. Should I thank Jesus for our situation?" I knew immediately he should not have said that—there were more crosses in that car than at the Vatican. It took five seconds for the car to stop and our little wet butts with our raggedy suitcases to be thrown out. I don't know if I was more mad or more proud of my brother for what he had done. Anyway, we were thumbing again.

As we kept walking, I could see we were approaching a farmhouse, and I said we will go to this house and tell the farmer that we're hungry and ask for some food. The sky was cloudy and looked like rain and maybe he would let us come in out of the bad weather. We hid our suitcases by the highway and began walking toward the farmhouse. We could see pigs eating and cows and horses grazing, which only made us hungrier. Most people know farmers usually have hound dogs. This farm was no different. The farmer was standing on his front porch with his three hounds next to him. When we got close to him, I yelled, "Good morning, Sir." He did not reply at all. I then said, "We are very hungry. Could you please let us have some food?" Again, no reply.

My brother made a great observation. He said to me, "This does not look good." We stopped walking just as a man said to the hound dogs, "Sick them." We turned around as the hounds charged toward us. The way they were barking you would have thought we were rabbits. When we got to the highway, they stopped. I don't know what would have happened if they caught us. The hounds we had would only bite a biscuit. As we stood at the highway, we noticed a young boy coming from the farm, carrying something we couldn't make out. As he approached us, we could see it was cornbread and pinto beans. He looked like the young boy that played the banjo in *Deliverance.* I looked back at the house and saw the Miss standing by the farmer. She waved at us. The young boy went back to the house. We sat on our suitcases and devoured the bread and beans. I guess we were now thirsty, but we could handle the thirst for a while.

Rides were easy, but these were usually farmers who were only going a few miles. We had to pass the time so I decided we would discuss the good and bad days we had with our Sweetie. We laughed when we remembered the day she had spanked our teacher. There were also the bad days, the days we didn't want to remember. On one occasion we were supposed to sing in front of the students and their parents. Everyone had turned out to hear the twins sing. I think we were 10 or 11 at the time of our appearances. Sweetie had said she would be sitting in the front row to give us encouragement on the day we were to sing. We were looking out from behind the stage waiting for her to arrive. Our appearances were postponed waiting for her to arrive, but she never did. My brother had panicked and would not sing until his mother arrived. She never did.

I finally persuaded him to sing with me and would hold his hand. We were supposed to sing "You Are My Sunshine." As we began to sing, he was doing OK. Then this man began pointing to us with a big grin on his face. My brother thought he was laughing at us, and he immediately began to cry. That was the end of our song. He kept crying as we stormed off the stage.

We learned our dad had something for her to do and would not let her attend our school performance. When I told my dad he should have let Sweetie come to the school and how disappointed that my brother was, he said, "I'm sure this won't be the last time he will be upset in his life." I saw how badly he cried. My dad's comment was, "Maybe I should have been there to give him something to cry about." I knew I had said enough.

I reminded my brother how she would play the piano while we sang songs. He began to cry a little so I put my arms around him and told him I would always take care of him. I became so angry at Sweetie, my father, and even myself because of what they had done to him and me being unable to heal his pain. We began thumbing again not really knowing where we were or how many miles we had to travel. When we would ask someone, their reply would be "You have a long way."

The Twins: Royce and Boyce

Our nights were pretty scary. We would sleep inside our suitcases and pray it didn't rain. The nights were really tough. There were frogs, snakes, armadillos, and rabbits but the only thing that bothered us the most were the ants. They were everywhere! I found a way of keeping them away from us. I took some of the food that was left and dug a hole and spread the food in the hole. This attracted them for a few hours. I knew I would have to devise a new plan the next day.

Chapter 10: Arriving in Houston

I knew I would have to find a way to take my brother's mind off Sweetie. I put him in charge of counting cars and trucks. I wanted him to tell me how many he had seen when we reached Houston. The nights were the hardest for him. The one thing that helped him was the chance he might be with his sister at the end of our third day. We were nearing Houston. We arrived on the outside of Houston and stopped at a gas station. We needed to go to the bathroom, so I went inside to get the key. The man asked if I was buying gas. I said, "No, but I need to use the bathroom." He wouldn't let me use it. He said, "It is only for people who buy gas." But then he saw what a couple of ragamuffins we were. He took pity on us. We still had $1.00 left, so we treated ourselves to two Babe Ruth candy bars and a Royal Crown Cola.

It finally dawned upon us that we had no idea how to find our sister. I assured my brother that I would find her, but first we had to find a place to live, and we needed a job. We finally arrived in Houston and the panic set in. We always thought Marlon was a big city until we saw Houston. As we were walking down the street, we stopped at a diner. They were advertising for a cook.

I left my brother outside and entered. I asked to see the manager. When he came out to see me, I told him I was applying for the job. The first words of his mouth were, "How old are you?" I quickly said, "16, nearly 17." He asked, "Do your parents know you are applying for this job?" I replied, "Of course they do." He noticed I kept looking outside. He turned to see what I was looking at and saw my brother.

I said, "Sir, my brother and I have hitched a long way. We have very little money and no place to stay. We have a sister who lives somewhere in Houston, but we don't know where." He said, "Go outside and get your brother." We both went outside, and he carried our suitcases to the back room. He said, "I know you are not 16, but I want to help you. You are definitely not a fry cook but I also need a dishwasher and a prep." I didn't have a clue what a prep was so I said, "I will take that." So, guess who became the dishwasher. Yep, my brother.

The manager said, "I know you do not have a place to stay. My neighbor has a garage apartment for rent. I will call him and ask if he will rent it to you." I asked, "When can we start work?" He said, "You just started."

You don't have to be a genius to wash dishes, but my brother thought it was the most important job in Houston. Our pay, if I can remember right, was $0.65 an hour for my brother and $0.70 for me. At the end of our first night, I asked Bob the manager for an advance. After he stopped laughing, he told me I sure had big ones for a kid. He drove us to the garage apartment where we met the owners. The rent was $10 a week, paid weekly. The apartment was within walking distance of the diner, so we had no problem getting to and from work.

The man who rented us the apartment wanted to know why we were alone. We told him we were waiting for our sister to arrive. We were working the same shift, so everything was fine until the day we started having separate shifts. My brother panicked. He didn't know how he could handle walking back and forth by himself, so for the next week I walked him to work and walked back to pick him up. His worst hours were at night. He so missed Sweetie and many nights he cried himself to sleep. I'd cried for him, but I never let him see me cry.

We were having the time of our lives. We had money. All of the girls loved us, and we could do what we wanted, but we knew there was something missing in our lives. It was Sweetie. Our clothes weren't exactly from Sears & Roebuck. As a matter of fact, most of our clothes had been made by Sweetie. The waitresses were wonderful. They did our clothes shopping and laundry, but I knew that things would not stay like this.

On June 19th we turned 14 and we thought we were men. One of the waitresses took me into the backroom and gave me a shot of whiskey. I thought I had fallen in love! All the attention we were getting at the diner helped my brother and I think of other things than our mom. There was one person at the diner that did not like us. She was the waitress that told us, "One day the state will discover you living alone in that garage apartment and make you both wards of the state." I didn't pay much attention to that. That was a mistake.

My brother was now more comfortable since we were back on the same shift. We arrived home one night, and the owner of the apartment was waiting to see us. He said, "Two people from the state stopped by checking on a tip that two young boys were living here alone. I told them that was not true, but I don't think they believed me." He told us to be careful. A couple weeks passed, and we forgot about it. Bad move.

One Saturday there was a knock at the door. Without thinking, my brother opened the door. There was a man and a woman standing there. When my brother saw who it was, he called me. The lady asked, "Are your parents home?" I told her, "They are working." She asked, "When will they be home?" "About 5:00 PM this afternoon," I replied. She indicated they would return at that time. We went to Mr. Martin's house, who was the owner of the apartment. I told him what had happened and when they would return.

Chapter 11: If We Only Knew...

"If we only knew our sister's address it would be so easy. The only thing I knew was her husband was in the Air Force." "Why didn't you tell me that?" We stayed at his house instead of our apartment that night and the next day he drove us to the Base and told them our story. He was sure they would be able to find our brother-in-law. We returned to the apartment, packed our clothes, and moved into Mr. Martin's home. Later that afternoon we were told we could no longer return to work. They were concerned that employing two underage workers would bring a fine.

Everything had been going so great, and now it was suddenly falling apart. We no longer had a job, no place to stay, and had not found our sister. The next morning we went to the Air Force Base. As we entered the gate the guard stopped us. We told him our situation. We were looking for my brother-in-law who was stationed there. He escorted us to the office of the Base Commander. We told them our problem, our name and where we could be reached. Mr. Martin said he would stay with us until we heard from our sister. We knew it wasn't possible to stay where we were. Hopefully our sister would try to find us.

Mr. Martin was so nice. He told us it would be impossible for us to stay with him the following week. We heard from the Base that our brother-in-law had been transferred to Tinker Air Force Base in Oklahoma City. They were nice enough to give us the number and information. To reach us Mr. Martin contacted the Base and explained our situation. We were told someone would be in touch with us in a few days. Waiting was really hard for my brother. I kept telling him everything would be fine, but just the idea of waiting and not hearing from anyone was the hard part.

Early one morning we received word from our sister Joanne. My brother was so excited he began to cry. She must have had 1,000 questions about how we arrived in Houston. We told her what had happened with Sweetie and our dad. She didn't seem surprised with what had happened.

Getting us to Oklahoma City was going to be a problem. She had no car. Mr. Martin said they would put us on the Trailways Bus to Oklahoma City. We could pay our own way from the money we earned from the diner. Riding a bus was new to us. I don't know why, but I felt more comfortable hitchhiking. I would talk about

Sweetie. My sister knew more about our mother than she would say at that time.

We decided to leave in two days, but until then we had to make sure the state did not find us. Mr. Martin dropped us off at the Trailways Bus station. It was early in the morning when we purchased our tickets. We told the ticket agent we wanted two tickets to Oklahoma City. We took our tickets and sat near the entrance where the buses loaded. My brother had to go to the bathroom, so I sat and waited. When he got back, we boarded the bus. He was so nervous about riding a bus such a long way.

We hadn't traveled 15 minutes when he fell into a deep sleep. I felt so bad for him. He rested his head on my shoulder before he fell asleep. He looked at me with tears in his eyes and said, "Do you think we will ever see our Sweetie again?" I turned my head away as tears ran into my eyes. I did not want him to see me crying. I replied, "Of course we will."

We never realized how long a trip it was. It seemed we stopped in every small town on the way thru Texas. People who never rode a bus years ago do not know what they have missed. There was no air, but you could leave the windows open. The engines were loud and smelly, the fumes were terrible, the bus stopped every couple 100 miles to allow passengers to stretch their legs and purchase something to eat. I think we purchased an O'Henry Candy Bar, a Peanut Pattie, and a Royal Crown Cola. We purchased the RC Cola because it came in a much larger size than a Coke.

It was amazing the things you can remember from your childhood. The trip was very tiring and rough. It seemed we stopped in every small town between

Houston and Oklahoma City. We were dirty. Our hair hadn't been combed for days, we smelled from perspiration, and we were beat.

We finally arrived in Oklahoma City late at night. I hoped we would recognize our sister since we hadn't seen her for some time. She also had neglected to tell us that she had a son. I guess he was about six or seven and he was a very polite little boy who never stopped talking. I soon found out why he called my sister's husband by his first name. He wasn't his father. Her husband drove her to pick us up. He was extremely nice and very handsome. We took our suitcases, put them in the trunk, and left the bus station. We stopped by the Air Base and dropped off her husband who had duty that night. I did not know she was getting divorced.

The Twins: Royce and Boyce

After he was dropped off at the Base we drove to her house. My brother, nephew, and I were sitting in the back seat. My sister was driving and turned and said, "I'm getting a divorce to marry another, Morris Caver." I now knew who the gentleman driving the car was. I had to admit he was very nice. We arrived at her home and our suitcases were put away. We sat down to talk. It seemed Morris had a big job with an oil drilling company in Oklahoma. He owned a home in Oklahoma City and as the conversation continued, we discovered that we would be moving into his house.

Chapter 12: The Separation

As we kept talking, I knew she was leading up to something. She finally said, "I can't take care of both of you boys. I saw the look on my brother's face as he began shaking. I told her we had never been separated in our life. I don't know if people understand the love and the bond twins have for each other. Sure, we fight, and we argue, but I think that only makes the love we have for each other stronger. I finally asked her "Do you know where Sweetie is?" She said, "I do." Thank goodness my brother had already gone to bed. She finally told me, "She is in Houston." I couldn't believe it. We were in the same town and never knew it. She did not want to see us yet. Her deserting us was still a thing she couldn't face.

I asked her, "Do you know where Corben is?" She said, "He is also in Houston." I told her "I don't know if I can leave my brother." I asked, "If you can't take care of the two of us, what are your plans?" She said, "We have an uncle (my brother Charles Houston) in the Army stationed near Ft. Smith, AR." I asked her, "Where is Ft. Smith?" She said, "It is across from Oklahoma." I asked her, "Please see if he can take care of the two of us." When she called him, I could see the look on her face and I knew he had said, "NO." She finally said, "We will discuss it tomorrow." I cried.

I knew my brother was not asleep. He turned to me with tears in his eyes and said, "We don't have a choice. At last, we have relatives to take care of us." I was surprised and it finally dawned upon me that maybe it was me who needed him more than him needing me. We cried ourselves to sleep that night knowing what had to be done. He would leave for Ft. Smith. We didn't see

each other for the next few years.

Chapter 13: The Reunion

I attended U.S. Grant High School in Oklahoma City, OK and he moved to Fort Smith, AR but we had an agreement. When we graduated high school both of us would join the Marines a year after graduation. He came to Oklahoma City, and we went to the Marine recruiting office. When we returned to our sister's house there was a strange car at her house. We noticed there were Texas plates on this car. We walked into the house. I couldn't believe my eyes. Sweetie was playing my sister's piano. Such a feeling came into my heart that I had never experienced before. We both saw her at the same time.

The love came shooting out of me and I forgave her for what she had done to us. My brother screamed,

"Sweetie," as he ran to embrace her. She had been to see my brother before seeing me. We sat and talked to her. The questions never stopped. "Why did you leave us?" "Where did you go?" "Why didn't you take us with you?" They just went on and on. She shared, "Your father had mistreated me so badly there was no other choice." Her new husband was a really nice man. I could see the love he had for her. She looked wonderful.

It never dawned on me to wonder if she had ever divorced my dad. She indicated they would be returning to Houston in a day or so. She was pleased I had joined the Marines. We saw her off the next day. She promised to keep in touch. My physical was taken, and my brother learned he had flunked his. I couldn't believe it. He told me, "I can try to enlist in the Army." He passed the physical and enlisted. I never knew why he was turned down in the first place.

The Twins: Royce and Boyce

I had three months before boot camp. I decided to find a job to have extra money. I went with my mother to Houston to work before I left. I applied to a company called *The Pig Stands.* Car hops would serve you in the car. No inside service. I was hired as a night manager back when no one asked for references. In Texas, at the time, as long as you could whistle and walk at the same time you were hired. I was closing one night and noticed a car had pulled in. I saw there was a woman about 50 and a girl my age.

I told them we were closing but I was happy to get anything for them. They told me they were on the way to Mexico to deliver costume jewelry. The older woman persuaded me to join them. I deducted what money I had coming and left a note that I quit, and we left. We were headed to Piedras Negras, Mexico. We crossed in from Eagle Pass, Texas. We spent two days trying to sell jewelry to people who had no money. At night the young girl would stay in a hotel, and we would sleep in the car. The older lady made me feel like I had died and gone to heaven.

One night as we were having a cerveza and this beautiful young girl kept looking at me. I went to where she was sitting. She performed a great dance. When I returned the two ladies had left. The bartender said they left me two words: "Adios Muchachos." I panicked. The young Mexican girl said I could stay with her. She wanted to marry me. For the next week I lived on Frijoles and tacos. You have to understand Mexicans are very dependent on beans.

There were about 30 ladies of the night all working for this one man. I discovered you can stay with a woman as long as you pay her. The Policia were looking for me because someone turned me in for not paying the lady I was staying with.

I was at the bar one evening. I met this American. I begged him to call my mother and tell her where I was. A week passed. I never heard from anyone. Then one night, as the Policia were trying to find me, I was watching and saw they had a picture of me. I wondered how they got that picture.

I came out and said, "That's me. I was handcuffed and taken to the la cárcel (jail). I was there for about two hours. They took me to a private room and there was my sister. My Mother had gotten in touch with her. I think I hugged her for an hour. She told me I stunk, and as soon as I could I immediately took a shower. They would say I smelled like third down and thirty.

Boyce Reginald Moudy

I had some time left before I reported to boot camp.

Chapter 14: The Grown Twins

I would see my brother from time to time. If we ever had leave at the same time we tried to take it so we could see each other. I could see he was changing. Every time we went for a drink, we usually had a fight with someone. I tried to talk to him about it, but he usually said, "You're the one that changed." He was sent to Vietnam later on and that really changed him. Unfortunately, he had two tours in that shithole. He rose in rank to warrant officer. I thought he would be sent home. The Army wanted to send him back for a third tour. He decided to retire after 18 years in the Army. He was discharged back to the states. He was a mess. Combat just destroyed him. He bounced around for years doing odd jobs. It seemed every time he met a woman in a bar he married her. He was married eight times. I once asked him, "Why don't you just live with them.?" His reply was, "That it was against God's will." I still laugh at that.

When I left the Marines I met a schoolteacher, Barb, and was married. She was from Boston, so we moved there. She even helped me take night classes at Harvard. For work, I went to work as a salesman for a beer and wine distributor. I worked my way up and became sale manager. Eight years later there was a corporate shake up and I lost my job. I told my wife we were moving to Florida. I was hired by a distributor as a sales manager. We had a home built in Temple Terrace outside of Tampa. I decided to open my own beer and wine distributorship.

The Twins: Royce and Boyce

By then my business had become very successful. I suggested my brother come to work for me driving a delivery truck. I was surprised when he accepted. The day he arrived in an old Ford camper he was a sight. He was drinking a Pearl beer and had two dogs in the front of the truck next to him. I told him he could stay at my house, but the dogs had to be boarded. He said he would sleep in the truck with the dogs. He worked for me a few months but was very short with the customers.

If only I had recognized his problems were from Vietnam. I didn't and I've always blamed myself.

Things were going well and one day he never came to work. He didn't call or leave a note, he just left. I discovered he had moved back to Texas and had remarried again. Her name was Erline, and she was wonderful. She was a widow with a small farm.

Chapter 15: Final Farewells

By this time, I was married with three children. I was determined my children would see Sweetie while she was living. I received a call from my brother that Sweetie was in the hospital with cancer of the uterus.

I took my children, and we flew to Houston. When we arrived at the hospital we rushed to see her. As I walked into her room, I stopped. I was not letting my children see this shriveled up lady. I made them stay outside while my brother and I sat beside her. I can't describe my feelings. Anger, I think. Royce was beside himself. My feelings for him went back to our childhood when I protected him. As we sat there, Sweetie left us. I cried both for my brother and Sweetie.

I returned home with my children and attempted to continue my life. Memories can be sweet and haunting. I had them both.

A couple years later I received a call from Erline, my sister-in-law. My brother was deathly ill. I left to see him with my family. The funeral parlor did a wonderful service. As I sat next to him before he passed, we sang the old songs our dad had sung to us, *Boys in Blue*, *Patania (The Pride of The Plains)* and our Favorite *Two Little Boys*. This is how our dad sang it to us. This is the song.

Two little boys had two little toys. Each had a wooden horse. Gaily they played each summer's day, Warriors both. Of course, one little chap then had a mishap and broke off his horse's head. He wept for his toy then cried with joy as his young little comrade said, "Don't you think Jack, I can see you crying when there's room on my horse for you? Climb up Jack. We'll soon be flying. He can go just as fast with two. When we grow up, we'll both be soldiers, and our horses won't be toys. Do you think that we'll remember when we were two little boys?"

The long years past, the war came at last, so daily they marched away. The cannons were loud. They met the mad crowd, while bleeding and dying Jack laid out with a cry. A horse flashed by out from the range so blue he galloped away to where Jack laid, his voice came strong and true. "Don't you think Jack, I can see you dying when there's room on my horse for two?

Boyce Reginald Moudy

Somehow Jack I'm all a tremble perhaps it's

the battle's noise, or perhaps it's I

remember when we were two little boys."

About the Author

Boyce Reginald Moudy lives in Sunny Florida. He has lived a life of adventure, raised three beautiful children, and was married to his wife Barb for over 20 years.

Boyce Reginald Moudy

He lived his life mostly between Boston and Tampa and after selling his beer and wine distributing company, lived a life of leisure until he met Sharon who owned a horse farm in Ocala, until her passing.

He now resides in Tampa, has been lucky enough to find love one more time, and enjoys daily walks, classical music, good jokes, a nice meal, and adventure. He said he has found the last love of his life.

www.ingramcontent.com/pod-product-compliance
Lightning Source LLC
LaVergne TN
LVHW041231080426
835508LV00011B/1147